THE AMERICAN LIMERICK BOOK

Also by Hugh Oliver and Keith MacMillan

The Canadian Limerick Book

THE AMERICAN LIMERICK BOOK

Hugh Oliver and Keith MacMillan
illustrated by Lorna Tomei

Beaufort Books, Inc.
New York Toronto

Library of Congress Cataloging in Publication Data

Oliver, Hugh, 1929–
  The American limerick book.

  1. Limericks.   2. Bawdy poetry.   I. MacMillan, Keith Campbell, 1920–
joint author.   II. Title.
PN6231.L5039   811'.07   80-21813
ISBN 0-8253-0001-0

Published in the United States by Beaufort Books, Inc., New York.
Published simultaneously in Canada by Nelson, Foster and Scott, Ltd.

Printed in the U.S.A.   First Edition
10   9   8   7   6   5   4   3   2   1

INTRODUCTION

Said Martin Luther, when charged with adding lasciviously to the music of his church (to whose glum elders all music was lascivious), "Why should the Devil have all the good tunes!"

Likewise we North Americans should muscle in on the English near-monopoly on good limericks, especially those inspired by provocative place-names:

"There was a young lady of Chichester . . ."

"There was a young lady of Cowes . . ."

"There was a young lady of Exeter . . ."

"There was a young lady of Buckingham . . ."

(or "Bucks" if you like to tackle these things head-on, as it were).

Yes, the English have been favored with their roster of titillating place names which has so inspired the limerick form.

But cannot their dominance be challenged? Why should they continue to have all the good limericks—or at least seem to have all the good limericks? On this side of the Atlantic can we not respond to the inspiration of such American place names as:

Biloxi,

Boise,
　Oahu,
　　Sheboygan,
　　　Tallahassee,
　　　Tuscaloosa,
　　　　(and let us not forget Intercourse, Pa.!)?
And Canadian:
　Batoche,
　　Chicoutimi,
　　　Metabechouan,
　　　　Saguenay,
　　　　　Saskatchewan,

Timiskaming,
　Toronto,
　　Vancouver?
Such typically North American names ought to prove irresistible to the inveterate limerick versificator, and so they have to us.

　　We protest too much, of course. Those brilliant verses of Ogden Nash for instance (". . . young belle of old Natchez") and other widely known ones like those by Eugene Field (". . . the bloody and murderous Sioux . . .") now have a secure and honored place in the all-time limerick repertoire. The present little collection of almost 300, mostly by ourselves (and patterned after those in its predecessor THE CANADIAN LIMERICK BOOK), is our modest response to the challenge of this hitherto almost all-English preserve.

The reader should also be aware that various states often have cities and towns of the same name, and where such happy coincidences occur, the authors' choice of state has been dictated by Solomon-like wisdom and a judicious flip of a coin.

The limerick's an art form complex, to be sure. Its contents run mainly, indeed irresistably, to sex. It is justly famous for virgins and masculine urgings and for a wide and raunchy vocabulary of sundry erotic effects. These characteristics have been dominant in the limerick since its emergence as "almost the only folklore of the intellectual"—a folklore solidly documented by Legman, Baring-Gould and others. Moreover, there is something in the North American ethos that encourages the flamboyantly violent (unconsciously no doubt) evident in many of these verses.

At the same time we have cherished the ideal of a certain nimbleness of verse. The lightly tickling feather is often more startling than the quick rapier or the swinging bludgeon.

But above all, we would like to think that our contribution will be as much stimulant as entertainment. The limerick is a participatory sport, whether to one-up somebody else or simply to have fun. So if you've a yen to compose, try some poetry rather than prose, with a giggle or grin as the habit creeps in (and it's easier than you'd suppose).

Hugh Oliver
Keith MacMillan

THE AMERICAN LIMERICK BOOK

ALABAMA

The repose that enclosed Alabama
Was disturbed by the ear-splitting clamor
    Of a maid being laid
    With the violent aid
Of a hit on the clit with a hammer.

H.O.

There is a young girl of Mobile
Whose hymen is made of chilled steel.
    To give her a thrill,
    Take a rotary drill
Or a number nine emery wheel.

Legman

A neurotic from north Tuscaloosa
Was afeared for his bride, lest he loosa,
    'Cause he hadn't the strength,
    Not to mention the length
That was sine qua non to enthoosa.
K.M.

ALASKA

A maiden who dwells in Galena
Has bubbies of graceful demeanor,
    And whenever she preens
    Those astounding poitrines
She insists upon Simoniz Kleener.

Legman

An Esquimau matron in Juneau
Is acknowledged as numero uno,
    For although her veneer
    Is a trifle severe,
She is only too anxious to . . . you know.

H.O.

A hot-blooded young Esquimau
Tried to screw his belov'd in the snau,
    But on finding it froze,
    He abruptly arose,
Saying, "If I can't come, I must gau."
H.O.

In the lands of the icy Northwest
Lived a maid with a dolorous breast;
    She had one nipple lost,
    Bitten off by the frost . . .
Or so she preferred to protest.
H.O.

ARIZONA

A Navajo maiden from Mesa
Was determined that nothing would phase her,
     Till a crafty old brave
     Thrust a spear in her cave
And provoked her to gush like a geyser.
                                        H.O.

An ignorant cowboy of Tucson
Thought it safe to have sex with a nucson,
     But the thing didn't work—
     Now he's saddled, poor jerk,
With a squaw with a little pappucson.
                                        K.M.

Said a rakish old father of Tucson
To his boy, "This is what you should ducson—
 When you're ready and hot,
 Shove it home on the spot
And you're sure to enjoy quite a fucson."
H.O.

An impetuous fellow from Yuma
Was attempting to ravish a puma,
 But gave up very quick
 Minus head, limbs and prick
And in obvious pain and ill-huma.
H.O.

ARKANSAS

A cop from the state Arkansas
Was seduced by a beautiful whas—
    Just because, so she said,
    She felt safer in bed
When she lay in the arms of the las.

H.O.

An effete poetaster of Corning,
From the moment he wakes in the morning,
    Is obscenely obsessed
    (He has often confessed)
By a passion for limerick porning.

K.M.

A dethigner who liveth in Fort Thmith
Ith without the equipment to pith,
    Generating debate
    On the quo of hith thtate,
Namely, ith he a man or a mith?
H.O.

A policeman of Little Rock, Ark,
Although frequently wide of the mark,
    Has a barrel of fun
    With his masculine gun,
As he blasts off his shot in the dark.
K.M.

CALIFORNIA

In that fun-loving state, California,
All the folks are undoubtedly hornia.
    Not even the dead
    Can be trusted in bed—
Which is simply to say that I'm warnia.

H.O.

A starlet from Beverly Hills
Used to walk about naked for thrills.
    Said a priest, "Though I blush
    When I look at her bush,
I will lift up mine eyes to the hills."

H.O.

In the fabulous land they call Disney
There's a dwarf who's all shriveled and wizney,
    'Cause from morning till night
    He's out making Snow White—
He's a lucky old ding-a-ling isney?

H.O.

An uncertain young lady of Fresno,
Who to most propositioners sesno,
    To a few of the guys
    I am told, she replies
With an eager, ambiguous, "Yesno!"

K.M.

At the corner of Hollywood-Vine
A voice in the crowd murmured "Fine!
    I've adjusted my drawers
    And I'm utterly yours,
But that snatch that you're at isn't mine."

H.O.

A delightful young maid of La Jolla
Lays around like the Malla of Golla,
    Hardly conscious, it seems,
    Of the copious streams
Of lascivious louts who enjolla.

H.O.

A voluptuous miss of La Jolla
Once complained to her lad, "I adolla,
    Yet you never drop in."
    He replied with a grin,
"Come around to my place and I'll sholla!"

K.M.

A New Yorker who moved to L.A.
On occasion was prompted to say
    That if he had guessed
    How debauched was the West,
He would not be committed to stay.

J.B.

Now Lucille from around Sacramento
(Her vagina a bit like a bent "O"),
Would incline to the left
As one entered the cleft,
But would writhe to the wright as she went "Oh!"
K.M.

On the beaches of warm San Diego,
Where the surfers both virile and gay go,
One can see ev'ry day
Such erotic display
That I think, come the summer, I may go.
K.M.

Said a girl from L.A., California,
"Yes the family really was bornia,
    'Cause our mum, being shrewd,
    Went a lot in the nude,
Making Daddy unsettled and hornia."
K.M.

"Please observe," said the youth of Los Angeles,
"How impressive my cock's erect angle is.
    In moments of zest
    It can tickle my chest—
That's pi radians more than its dangle is."
R.A.M.

A recluse from around Pasadena,
Being served with a paltry subpoena,
    Dropped the thing in the john
    And assumed thereupon
A remote, uncompliant demeanor.

K.M.

A gaudy young girl of Pomona
Does her act in a sexy kimono;
    She tastefully ripples
    Her tumescent nipples
With lipstick around the coronae.

K.M.

Said a dullard of old San Francisco,
"I can't figure it out—where does this go?"
    "Well," she said, "I've a space,
    But be sure, when in place,
Let the other, instead of the piss go."

K.M.

Said a freaky French frier of Frisco,
"I do all my deep frying with Crisco,
    Which entices the girls
    More than rubies, or pearls,
Or those dry little things from Nabisco."

K.M.

A girl from around Santa Cruz
Just doesn't know how to refuz,
    And to satisfy more
    Of the men at her door
She will often accept them in tuz.
H.O.

A sodomist jailed in San Quentin
Is broodin' and darkly repentin'
    The lack, in this nation,
    Of sex education—
To blame for the wrong way he went in.
H.O.

This broad from around Santa Rosa
Is a hot-box, and every one knowsa.
    When she swims in the nude,
    Screaming out to be scrude . . .
Well you don't so much ridesa as rowsa.
H.O.

COLORADO

There's a rabbit in high Colorado
Who will cringe all the day in the shadow
    But at night will bestow,
    On some trembling doe,
All the frenzy of pent-up bravado.
K.M.

Said a wife, as they drove out of Boulder,
"Now, before you become any older,
    I believe you should know
    You're becoming quite slow" —
So he stopped on the shoulder and roulder!
K.M.

A prospector who dwelt in Fort Morgan
Had his cock turned to rock by a gorgon,
  Although not by her style
  Nor the guile in her smile,
But the hex of her sexual organ.

H.O.

A devious lad from La Junta
Decided it might be quite funta
  Be hermaphrodite.
  As he said with delight,
"I can screw me whenever I wunta!"

H.O.

A ferocious young plumber of Boulder
Argued hotly his girl had grown colder,
  And in making his point
  He created a joint
By annointing his foreskin with solder.
H.O.

'T was a hot-blooded student of Denver
Who developed a passionate yenver
  A delicious co-ed
  Who would murmur in bed,
"There are things that I simply won't stenver."
K.M.

CONNECTICUT

A ninety-year diehard from Norwich
Consumed a whole tureen of porrich,
    But his subsequent claim
    Of the ten times he came
Hasn't ever been proved, to my knowlich.
H.O.

A shady young lady of Vernon
Reposed her voluptuous sternon
    A pneumatic drill
    And, with consummate skill,
She discovered the ultimate turnon.
H.O.

There was a brave girl of Connecticut
Who flagged the express with her petticut,
    Which critics defined
    As presence of mind
But deplorable absence of ecticut
Ogden Nash

I once knew a guy from Connecticut
In behavior bereft of all ecticut.
    Who would strip to the nude
    The most reticent prude . . .
I dunno if he could, but he secticut.
K.M.

A compulsive young marksman from Groton,
When he found he'd a hell of a hot-on,
    Simply triggered his sights
    On a pair of pink tights
And from twenty-five yards hit them spot on.
H.O.

DELAWARE

At Rehoboth a broad on the beach
Lay stretched out in the sun—out of reach,
    Till a treacherous hand
    Burrowed up through the sand . . .
And in Texas they blanched at the screech.

H.O.

Said a prissy young missy of Delaware
To her panting young men, "I am well aware
    You're for contact direct,
    But since you're erect,
Put on this, which I make ev'ry fella wear."

K.M.

An embarrassed young bridegroom of Dover
So frustrated his bride that he drove her
    Clean out of her mind:
    His before lay behind
And nothing would make him turn over.

H.O.

DISTRICT OF COLUMBIA

In Washington city, D.C.,
There are wonders around you to see—
    The historical page
    Of our great heritage,
But it's hard to find somewhere to pee.
H.O.

The sex of the rex in the White House
Was standing erect as a lighthouse,
    And the band grit its teeth
    Playing "Hail to the Chief"—
After all, it is such a polite house!
H.O.

FLORIDA

A flowery young flossie of Florida,
As the weather was getting much torrida,
    Took off all her clothes
    From her neck to her toes,
And was mad when the locals ignorrida.

J.B.

An impatient old spinster in Florida
Whose dreams grew progressively torrida
    Leapt onto a 'gator
    In hopes that he'd mator;
But nothing so crude—he just swollida.

H.O.

There's a town in the South, Chattahoochee,
Where they still do the old hootchie-kootchie
    With a good deal of pride
    (Rather unjustified,
In the view of this hardened debauchee).

K.M.

There was an old dame of Fort Pierce
Whose sexual jollies were fierce,
    Appertaining to guys
    With some kinky supplies
That would never be offered at Sears.

K.M.

An electrical man of Fort Myers
Is convinced that the secret is wires,
    And will try to seduce
    Them with low-voltage juice
As they placidly play with his pliers.

K.M.

I have heard of a girl in Key Largo
Who imposes a sort of embargo
    On incontinent men
    If they grunt now and then
As they try to deliver their cargo.

K.M.

An impatient young man of Key West,
When he first put his tool to the test,
    Was impelled by such speed
    To get on with the deed
That he came before getting undressed.
H.O.

I recall a hot lass of Key West
Who did all that she wanted, with zest,
    And when progeny came,
    That remarkable dame
Had quadruplets, i.e. two abreast.
K.M.

A Goliath of Pine Island Sound
Had a dong that would drag on the ground,
    So he carried it high,
    Unconstrained by a fly,
Wound around . . . and around . . . and around . . .

K.M.

There's a girl from around Tallahassee
Who is quite an outstanding young lassie,
    Which description pertains
    Not to talent or brains
But the shape of that neat, classy chassis.

K.M.

GEORGIA

A lady from way down in Ga.
Became quite a notable fa.
    But she faded from view
    With a quaint I.O.U.
That she signed "Miss Lucrezia Ba."
Lure of the Limerick

There was once a pale frail of Augusta,
So neurotic that everything fusta,
    And she longed for a good
    Kind magician who would,
With a wave of the wand, readjusta.
K.M.

An entrancing young girl of Savannah
Would parade in a skimpy bandannah.
    A sculptor came by—
    She gave him the eye,
So he got out his tool and begannah.
K.M.

There's a frigid young lady of Smyrna
Who will not be turned on, so to turn her,
    An importunate squire
    Almost set her on fire
By inserting a large bunsen burner.
H.O.

To her daughter a lady from Tate
Had suggested her sex life should wait,
    Unaware she'd been laid
    By the fire brigade;
So her tete-a-Tate came much too late.

H.O.

HAWAII

A flatulent nun of Hawaii
One Easter eve supped on papaya,
    Then honored the Passover
    By turning her ass over
And obliging with Handel's "Messiah."
Lure of the Limerick.

From the seashore a lady of Hilo
Paddled out with her arms on a lilo.
    A triangular fin
    Swam beneath with a grin . . .
Now she's known as the Venus de Milo.
H.O.

A flowery young maid from Kailua
Would prefer to be playful than pua,
    But went to excess
    When she stripped off her dress
And invited the townsfolk to scrua.
H.O.

Said a worldly old broad of Oahu
To her daughter, "I hated your pa who
    Tried to bolster his 'id'
    With the things that he did
As a horny, detestable yahoo!"
K.M.

IDAHO

There's a jock down in south Pocatello
Who's convinced he's a hell of a fellow,
    For his wife gives him free,
    (And so copiously!)
What she learned in a Texas bordello.
K.M.

An impotent man of Twin Falls
Was treated with racehorses' balls,
    Which so cured his weakness,
    He entered the Preakness
And screwed all the mares in their stalls.
H.O.

A boisterous beauty of Boise
In sex is exceedingly noise.
    In moments of passion
    Her raptures Parnassian
Are heard from Seattle to Joise.
                  K.M.

A frustrated female from Burley,
On finding her mate had come early,
    Laid her hand on an axe
    And with one or two whacks
Soon reduced him to one short and curly.
                H.O.

ILLINOIS

An Indian chief of Chicago
Was the first to invent the embago
    On trade with the whites
    And especially at nights—
When they asked would he please let his squago.
K.M.

There's a girl from La Harpe, Illinois,
Who is hung on this guy from Detroit
    With his bold "savoir faire"
    And his "air solitaire"
Not to mention his "je na sais quoi."
K.M.

A pederast here in Moline
In search of a new sort of scene
　　A broad tried to lay,
　　But she answered, "No way!
I happen to know where you've been."
H.O.

Said a tardy young man of Decatur
To his girl ev'ry time he would date her,
　　"Now we're here on the bed,
　　You proceed on ahead,
And I'll do what I can to come later."
K.M.

An impotent person of Pekin
Discovered his ballocks were leakin',
    Which reduced the amount
    Of his seminal count
From millions to hardly worth speakin'.

H.O.

A mechanic who hailed from Peoria,
To his girl said, "I fondly adoria.
    Could you lower your pants,
    'Cause I'd relish the chance
Just to measure the depth and the boria."

K.M.

A lass from Peru, Illinois,
Was suffused with a feeling of joy
    When she found that the place
    Of that feminine "space"
Was outstanding when part of a boy.

K.M.

INDIANA

There was once a young girl from Fort Wayne,
Who would relish it now and again.
    I had better explain
    About "now and again"—
I mean NOW, and AGAIN and AGAIN . . . !

Anon

A wretched young man from La Porte
Was hung much too thin and too short,
    So he largened his shaft
    With an elephant graft
And now it won't fit where it ort.

H.O.

A wet-nurse who services Gary
Has a bosom both massive and hairy.
    Nonetheless, since eighteen
    She's provided a clean
And productive, and portable, dairy.

K.M.

There was once a young maiden of Muncie,
Of mentality simple and duncie,
    But with bubbies and ass
    So unique of their class
She was eager to let everyuncie.

K.M.

A compliant young girl of South Bend,
Ever eager to follow the trend,
     Was invited to screw
     At an orgie or two
But was soon tuckered out—in the end.

K.M.

'Twas a bride just outside Terre Haute
Who announced to her spouse, and I quaute,
     "You should know I decline
     To perform '69'
Plus some others I will not denaute."

K.M.

A youth from the town Terre Haute
Fell madly in love with a stoat,
    But had cause for regret
    When he tried on his pet
Some tricks he'd observed in "Deep Throat."

H.O.

IOWA

A demanding young lady from Boone
Intimated her coming quite soon,
    Which brought some relief
    To her consort beneath,
Who'd been up her the whole afternoon.
H.O.

A musical man of Dubuque,
When he wrote his ninth Prelude and Fuque
    Was constrained to observe
    As he steadied his nerve,
"If I do this again, I will puque!"
K.M.

A neurotic young man of Des Moines
Is incessantly taut in the groines,
'Cause the feminine limb
Is a fetish with him,
And especially the part where they joines.

K.M.

Said a thoughtful young man of Des Moines,
"When I think of the fruit of my loines,
Either whitish or yellow,
It's hard for a fellow
To know if he's coming or goines."

J.G.

Says a lecher who lives in Sioux City,
"I've a passion for nibble and titty,
    And on Saturday night
    Take a special delight
Getting down to the real nitty-gritty!"

K.M.

KANSAS

A tight-end receiver from Hays
Has lusted about it for days;
    And on clasping his hands
    Round and broad in the stands
Made a touchdown in less than two plays.

H.O.

The career of a man in Topeka
As a chauvinist stud and self-seeker
    Was exploded one night
    When his girl put him right
As to which of the sexes was weaker.

K.M.

An experienced lecher from Mission
Was describing the arts of coition.
　　Said an aging old pop.
　　"I just lays down on top."
Cried the lecher, "A brand new position!"
H.O.

KENTUCKY

There was an old gent from Kentuck
Who boasted a filigreed schmuck,
    But he put it away
    For fear that one day
He might put it all in and get stuck.

Legman

A fragile neurotic from Murray
Was plagued by the terrible worry
    That if he should cough
    His balls would drop off.
And he did. And they did. End of story.

H.O.

54

A lusty old lecher of Murray
Must always make love in a hurry.
    "Well I has to," he said,
    "They near jumps through the bed
When they feels that me dingle is furry!"
K.M.

The fellows who work in Fort Knox
Have gold flowing out of their cocks;
    And the ladies, behold,
    Go out panning for gold
Using methods quite heterodox.
H.O.

LOUISIANA

In New Orleans there dwelled a young Creole
Who, when asked if her hair was all reole,
　　Replied with a shrug,
　　"Just give it a tug
And decide by the way that I squeole."
Lure of the Limerick

An uncouth lusty youth of the Creoles,
I'll admit is a bit of a heole;
　　He assesses a prude
　　By her mood in the nude
And a bitch by the pitch of her squeole.
K.M.

A barman in bored Bogalusa
Poured drinks for a dame to amusa.
    For one of his tricks
    He used nitro mix . . .
And the bomb squad was called to defusa.
H.O.

There was an old man of Lake Charles
Who would keep all his bourbon in barles
    In a place out behind
    Which his boys couldn't find—
Thus engendering family quarles.
K.M.

The harlots who serve Natchitoches
Paint daffodils all round their crotches,
    Which does nothing to
    The guys in situ
Though it pleases the voyeur who watches.
H.O.

A well-hung young man from Tallulah
Spanned the length of a twenty-inch ruler.
    Then this daring old soul
    Sort of swallowed him whole
And it bloody near burst her uvula.
H.O.

MAINE

An adventurous lady of Maine
Had a yen to be screwed by a train.
    And on lifting her dress
    To a passing express
Was, alas, never heard of again.

H.O.

A superior lady of Maine
Though seducible now and again,
    When removing her clothes,
    Would wrinkle her nose
With a maddening air of disdain.

K.M.

A furtive old fellow from Bath
Occasioned his mistress's wrath;
    On commencing to harden
    He entered her garden
But led it up quite the wrong path.

H.O.

The desirable ladies of Brewer
Became fewer, and fewer, and fewer,
    Till on one sorry day
    There was only one lay—
And she wouldn't let anyone screw her.

H.O.

There was a young lady of Dexter
Whose husband exceedingly vexed her,
    For whenever they'd start
    He'd unfailingly fart
With a blast that damn nearly unsexed her.

Legman

MARYLAND

The boobs of a beauty in Easton
Hung out for admirers to feast on,
    And would gracefully rise
    For a few of the guys,
Like the tips of her tits had some yeast on.
H.O.

A vindictive old fellow from Laurel
Got involved in a family quarrel;
    So he picked up his knife
    And castrated his wife
And some other things highly immoral.
H.O.

MASSACHUSSETS

There was once a young girl of Cape Cod
Who thought babies were fashioned by God;
    But 'twas not the Almighty
    Who lifted her nightie—
'Twas Roger the lodger, the sod!
Anon.

There was once an old bawd from Cape Cod,
Who, when tourists would ask, "have you scrod?",
    Would reply, "Goddam right!
    Up to ten ev'ry night!"
There's a gutsy, pluperfect old broad!
K.M.

It's a habit of husbands of Salem
When their wives (or their mistresses) failem,
To go slightly berserk,
And if that doesn't work
Then to leap on the bed, and impalem.

K.M.

There was a young man from Wood's Hole
Who had an affair with a mole.
Though a bit of a nancy
He *did* like to fancy
Himself in the dominant role.

Lure of the Limerick

A slothful young fellow from Hull,
When life seemed excessively dull,
    Once tried thinkful wishin'
    With slow manumission—
But dropped off to sleep in a lull.

K.M.

The Reverend Archbishop of Lynn
Was suddenly tempted to sin.
    But an angel of God
    Put a hex on his rod
Thus preventing him getting it in.

H.O.

MICHIGAN

An animal trainer I knew
Is in love with a nice kangaroo,
 So he pockets his pride
 As they live there inside
Of the tolerant Kalamazoo.
K.M.

This widow who's living in Michigan—
You can tell when she's gettin the itchigan
 From the flush of her skin
 And the sphinxian grin
Of the postman who's filling her nichigan.
H.O.

We lament that old drunkard of Michigan
As he fought to sustain his last wishigan.
    Not a drop did he waste
    As he died, undisgraced—
"I refushe absholutely to pishigan!"
K.M.

A peculiar young man of Detroit
Was agreed to be quite maladroit.
    After doughnuts and tea
    He would relish a pee
With a ring on his thing, like a quoit.
K.M.

A typist in Kalamazoo
Who relished an old-fashioned scroo
    Was aroused by her boss
    To coitus in os—
So a blow-job she blatantly bloo!
H.O.

MINNESOTA

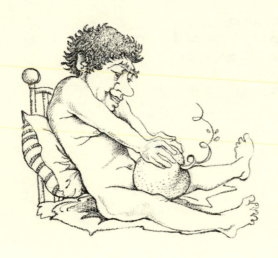

Said an artist of fame from Anoka,
"Yes, I color my weapon with ochre
  'Cause my wife's, so to speak,
  A banana-mad freak,
And she fancies it is when I poke her."

H.O.

To an elegant lad of Duluth
The vagina was hot and uncouth,
  So he took to his bed
  Mushy melons instead,
And so spent the best part of his youth.

K.M.

Said a shoemaker up in St. Paul,
To his eager, vivacious young doll,
   "Until Fridays are past
   I must stick to my last,
But on weekends I'll give you my awl."
K.M.

Said a passionate girl of St. Paul,
"When I think of your pendulous baul
   And that member erect
   I get hot to connect,
And *to hell* with preventive withdraul!"
K.M.

During foreplay, a youth from Duluth
Got excited and lost a front tooth;
    And when deep in situ
    He was bitten in two—
Which should teach him to be so uncouth!

H.O.

Said a pro from Roseau, Minnesota,
"Well I really don't care an iota
    If they call me unkind
    When I fuck them all blind,
In achieving my annual quota."

K.M.

There was once a young man of St. James
Who indulged in the jolliest games:
    He lighted the rim
    Of his grandmother's quim
And laughed as she pissed through the flames.

Legman

MISSISSIPPI

There was once a young girl of Biloxi
Who protested, "I'm nobody's doxi,
    Though a party that swings
    Will provoke me to things
I would never let Benjamin Spoxi!"
K.M.

There was a young belle of old Natchez
Whose garments were always in patchez.
    When comment arose
    On the state of her clothes,
She drawled, "When Ah itchez, Ah scratchez."
Ogden Nash

There was a young lady of Natchez
Who chanced to be born with two snatches.
    And she often said, "Shit!
    I would give either tit
For a man with equipment that matches."

Legman

A man in the town Picayune
Lay restlessly watching the moon.
    As the cats came to life,
    He remarked to his wife,
"I perceive they are playing our tune."

H.O.

MISSOURI

There's a maid from the town Olivette
Who has played much too tricky to get;
    But although eighty-four
    She is still fairly sure
She will lose her virginity yet.
H.O.

There was a young lad from St. Louis
Who was raised much too much ingenouis,
    But when puberty called
    He was lustily balled
And is now much too cocky and scrouis.
K.M.

There was a young man of Missouri
Who fucked with a terrible fury
    Till hauled into court
    For his bestial sport,
And condemned by a poorly hung jury.
Legman

A nun from the town of Creve Coeur
Was extremely confused, as it were,
    When, from one point of view
    She attempted to do
Unto him what he did unto her.
H.O.

MONTANA

A fastidious youth from Montana
Would undress in an elegant mana,
    And for sex would prepare,
    Cleaning teeth, combing hair
(Head and pubic) before he begana.
K.M.

There was once a young lady of Butte
Who was rather obsessively cutte;
    She perfected a pink
    Little vaginal wink
That was simply *too! too!*—and she knutte.
K.M.

An exciting young dentist of Billings
Gets the girls by the depth of his drillings.
    When he says, "Open wide,"
    They are well satisfied
(On the hole) with emergency fillings.
K.M.

A resolute rabbi from Miles
Impressed all the local gentiles
    With his power of belief
    When he bent with his teeth
And circumcised all of his piles.
H.O.

A filthy old man of Helena
Regressed from obscene to obscena.
   What he did I won't say,
   But included fowl play
With a turkey, two tits and a wiena.

H.O.

There was once a young girl of Missoula
Whose Lothario thought he could foola
   As he moistened her lips
   Undulating her hips
Just to teach her (he said!) how to hula.

K.M.

NEBRASKA

When I saw this young girl from Nebraska,
I was seized with the urge to unmaska.
    As to how she would feel
    If I asked her to peel,
I admit Idaho—but Alaska!
K.M.

A charming young maid from McCook
Was molested one night by a spook.
    But such interaction
    Brought no satisfaction—
'Twas unable to touch, only look.
H.O.

A supine young lady in Ewing
Was curious what he was doing
    As he rocked to and fro
    On her fulcrum below,
So she asked, "Are you gumming or gooing?"
                      H.O.

A lustful young lass from O'Neill
Expressed a strong preference for eel.
    She said "My pet conger
    Is half a yard longer
And doesn't go limp on the the deal."
                H.O.

NEVADA

A pretentious young man of Nevada
Boasted loud to his girl, once he'd hada
    "You get only the best!"
    But she wasn't impressed
And with irony murmured, " . . . de nada!"
K.M.

A flatulant fairy from Carson
Was forever impaling his arse on
    Some handy old pole,
    And once, save his soul,
He found he had sat on the parson.
H.O.

A wistful young maiden from Reno
Was anxious to have a bambino;
    And when she succeeded
    The menfolk all pleaded
"It must have been him. But not me. No!"
H.O.

NEW HAMPSHIRE

A shy little student from Derry
Got stoned on two glasses of sherry.
    And then her professor
    Began to undress her—
And was she responsive? Oh *very*!
H.O.

A lustful young student from Keene,
Although she was only fifteen,
    Had encountered the tool
    Of each boy in the school
And some members of staff in between.
H.O.

NEW JERSEY

The virgin he raped in New Jersey
Occasioned him some controversy.
    French tourist, sixteen;
    And what did she mean
When she looked in his eyes, and said "Mercee!"?

H.O.

A blue-eyed young beauty from Closter
Was number one lay on his roster;
    And while occupied
    With those on the side
He would keep her on ice, then defroster.

H.O.

There was an old man in Fort Lee,
Exceedingly anxious to pee;
    And the crowd gave a shout
    As he splashed it about.
There was an old man—it was me!
H.O.

NEW MEXICO

A cook from the town Albuquerque
Took pleasure in stuffing a turque;
    Not the old-fashioned way,
    With some parsley and bay—
But straight up it, and certainly quirque!

H.O.

A careless young fellow from Hobbs
Was blessed with a couple of knobs;
    And with two girls each lay,
    It is proper to say
That he risked being caught on the jobs.

H.O.

A girl from around Sante Fé
Was a hell of a wonderful lé;
    She would practice coition
    In any position
And willingly do it all dé.

H.O.

An immaculate lady of Taos
Had her panties trimmed neatly with laos,
    But a vulgar young man
    Raped her roughly and ran,
And left them pure panties in chaos.

Legman

NEW YORK

An indecent young lass of Batavia,
When jailed for indecent bahavia,
  Quite unsettled the guard
  With a husky "Get hard
As I slowly and madly depravia!"

K.M.

There's a gal at the zoo in the Bronx
With a liking for lions and monx;
  And she goes rather ape
  For a species of rape
That involves all the elephants' tronx.

K.M.

A precocious young girl of Batavia,
Widely known for outlandish behavia,
    As her boyfriend withdrew
    Giggled, "Over to you
With that ring on your ding I just gavia."
K.M.

Said an amateur hooker of Broadway,
"Though I'm happy to make it the mod way,
    I would like to begin
    An *original* sin—
Or at least to invent a new odd way."
K.M.

Said a roué from old Canandaigua
To his partner, "My God! What a haigua!"
    She replied with harangues
    And a baring of fangs—
Then she bit off his cock, like a jaigua.
R.A.M.

There was once a young lady of Corning
Who would climax without any warning;
    But delay it she could
    (And was *ever* so good)
If aroused about 5 a.m.
K.M.

An exhausted young man from Dunkirk
Was unable to get it to work.
    With his hand on his thing
    He knew well how to cling
But he hadn't a clue how to jerk.

H.O.

A perverted old man of Fredonia
To the girl he was with, said "If onia
    Weren't so wholesome and fresh
    When we touch in the flesh!
But my jollies I'll get when I phonia!"

K.M.

A feminist whore of New York
Soon put herself quite out of work
    When, disgruntled with men,
    Crying, "Never again!"
She just bunged herself up with a cork.
                                    K.M.

A lad from Niagara Falls
Had a pair of spectacular balls
    Which he kept in condition
    For non-stop emission—
Inspired, no doubt, by the Falls.
                                    K.M.

A despoiling young lad of Poughkeepsie
Would encourage a girl to get tipsy,
    Whereupon he'd display,
    I am sorry to say,
All the moral restraint of a gypsy.
                                    K.M.

A voluptuous maiden of Queens,
As she passed through her turbulent teens
    Grew incredibly cool
    At the beach or the pool—
And unbearably hot in the jeans.
                                    K.M.

She will stroll on the sidewalks of Rochester
And whisper to men, "Buenos noches, sir."
    As they pivot about
    With their tongues hanging out
She will laugh as she watches their crotches stir.

H.O.

Said a stupid young girl of Schenectady
Of her boyfriend, "I never expectady
    Would suggest we recline
    After dinner and wine,
And I still wonder why in the hectady."

K.M.

NORTH CAROLINA

A well-endowed fellow of Dunn
Has ballocks that each weigh a ton;
    And the size 'round his flies
    Is a nasty surprise
To the ladies, who turn tail and run.
H.O.

A cheeseparing skinflint from Graham
Had rogered two whores but won't pay 'em,
    So they took him in hand
    Nearly murdered him, and,
As the judge said, "...commited sweet mayhem."
H.O.

A lascivious lady of Raleigh,
Much in love with the pole of a traleigh,
    Has some unorthodox
    But sensational shocks
To enliven her sexual faleigh.
                                        K.M.

NORTH DAKOTA

Said a cute statistician of Bismarck,
"Will I note the admission of his mark
    To my delicate clit
    As a definite hit,
Or just fill out my form with a quiz mark?"
K.M.

There was a young lady of Mott,
Who inserted a fly up her twat
    And pretended the buzz
    Was not what it was,
But something she knew it was not.
Legman

A thoughtless old fellow from Ray,
Near the climax of sexual play,
    Impromptu elected
    To be well vasected—
Which caused quite a bit of delay.

H.O.

A crafty old preacher in Ray
inveigled a choirboy one day
    Way down in the crypt;
    And when they were stripped
He gently intoned, "Let us play."

H.O.

A reluctant young lady from Mandan
Tried to shift what he'd gotten his hand on;
    But after some stroking,
    He soon had her smoking
In flaming and lustful abandon.

H.O.

OHIO

A provoking young lady of Canton
Causes women and clergy to rant on,
    For they cannot condone
    What she does, when alone
With a guy, and with nary a pant on.
K.M.

A widow who lived in Celina
Made every man lust who had seen her.
    But a neighbor revealed
    He had ploughed through her field,
And his verdict—the ass wasn't greener.
H.O.

There was a young lady of Sycamore
Who wanted her boyfriend to prycamore,
 Indicating the last
 Time he came much too fast,
And she didn't enjoy such a quycamore.

H.O.

An obsessive old man of Toledo
Is sustained by the tedious credo
 That the functional aim
 Of a beautiful dame
Is to bolster his fading libido.

K.M.

There's a group in around Cincinnati
Who assure us that sex doesn't matter;
    Though their girls in the spring
    May be thin as a string,
Come the fall, will be bulging and fatter.
K.M.

A retiring old fellow of Dayton
Has begun to lose interest in matin',
    And his wife, bless her soul,
    Suffers loss of control,
Being hotly frustrated from waitin'.
K.M.

A straightforward matron of Stow
Was distressed by her kinky old beau,
    And bunged up each channel
    With wads of thick flannel,
Saying, "Now he has nowhere to go!"
H.O.

OKLAHOMA

Requiring a condom in Moore,
The G.I. rushed into a store.
    "No, not Durex", he said,
    "Gimme Pyrex instead—
I gotta hot dish out the door."
H.O.

A contortionist near Seminole
Liked to dilate her twat like a bole,
    And when she began,
    Her randy young man
Didn't know from a head in the hole.
H.O.

A degenerate madam of Tulsa
Was so vast that no man dared repulsa
    Save a parson who could,
    And who frequently would
In libidinous orgy, convulsa.
K.M.

There was once a young girl of Eugene
Whose response was excessively mean.
    Though she was, they all said,
    Rather stingy in bed,
She at least was dependably clean.

K.M.

Two girls on the top of Mt. Hood.
Said the good girl, "It's hard to be good."
    Said the bad, with a shriek
    As she squirmed on the peak,
"It has *gotta* be hard to be good!"

H.O.

OREGON

"I would love," said the lady of Oregon,
"To revert to professional whoregon,
    Were it not that my spouse
    Would disown me, the louse,
A conclusion I take to be foregone."
K.M.

Dismounting a maid in Astoria
The youth lay in blissful euphoria.
    As she climbed out of bed,
    He restrained her and said,
"You come back here. I want a lot moria."
H.O.

An eccentric young man of Ontaria
Once announced to his genital varia,
    "I have knitted this red
      Woolly snood for your head,
With a pocket for each of the paria."
K.M.

PENNSYLVANIA

An impatient young man of Altoona
Comes to climax, like others, but soona;
    When meeting his date
    He can't seem to wait
And will get all excited, and roona.
K.M.

A provoking young girl from Bryn Mawr,
When seduced in the back of a cawr,
    To the gentleman said,
    "It's not much, as a bed,
But it's better than standing, by fawr."
K.M.

A statistical fellow of Erie
Made his clients decidedly leery
    When he found that his pals
    Rated more than the gals,
In response to his poll-taking query.
K.M.

This friend that I knew would guffaw
When his aunts and his sisters and Ma
    Would evasively say,
    "We're from Lancaster way—"
(They were really from Intercourse, Pa.)
K.M.

A recluse of Du Bois, Pennsylvania,
Has developed a positive mania
    For shoemakers' awls
    And pawnbrokers' balls
And other symbolic extrania.

K.M.

A fastidious dandy from Milton
Would complain that his trousers got spilt on.
    "Well in future," she said,
    "When you leap into bed
I suggest that you come with a kilt on."

H.O.

Vowed a gallant of old Philadelphia
To his bride, "I will battle through helphia!"
    But alas, with the dawn
    And the honeymoon gone,
They prefer easy living on welphia.
K.M.

Superpimp, as he combed Philadelphia,
Told recruits, "I'll get out there and selphia!
    And to live like a duchess,
    Just give them as muchess
They ask, and their penises swelphia."
R.A.M.

A curious maiden from Plum
Was either naive or plain dumb.
    To her boyfriend's surprise
    When he opened his flies
She remarked, "You have misplaced your thumb."
H.O.

Though this butcher around Punxsutawney
Seems to us kind of wizened and scrawney,
    All the ladies adore
    Just to visit his store
For a piece of his special balawney.
K.M.

An annoying old voyeur of Scranton
Goes about in the parks with a lant'n
    Which he shines in the eyes
    Of the gals and the guys
At the height of their writhin' and pantin'.

K.M.

A babe from the town Susquehanna
Failed to come when she tried a banana;
    But responding quite well
    To her failure, said "Hell,
As a baby I'm only a larner."

H.O.

RHODE ISLAND

The Right Reverend Archbishop of Foster
Sidled up to this babe to accost her,
    And was quick to agree
    On a suitable fee—
Two Hail Marys and one Paternoster.
                  H.O.

A well-endowed lecher of Warwick
Left his architect mistress eupharwick,
    "Not because of the size,"
    She remarked with surprise,
"But your column—decidedly Darwick."
                  H.O.

SOUTH CAROLINA

A young aesthete from South Carolina
Had a penis that tinkled like china,
    But while shooting his load
    It cracked like old Spode,
So he bought him a Steuben vagina.

Legman

A liberal lady from Greer,
Presenting her opulent rear,
    Was pained to discover
    Her hard-driving lover
Was ignorant where he should steer.

H.O.

An ailing young fellow from Cayce
Tried actively hard to keep pace,
    And one lusty night,
    With squeals of delight
He vanished right up without trace.

H.O.

SOUTH DAKOTA

A medical student from Burke
Had a tackle that just wouldn't work.
    Though luscious and massive,
    Could only stay passive
And drove every night-nurse berserk.
H.O.

'Twas an odd sort of broad in Pierre,
Who preferred it with *everything* bare,
    And even professed, it
    Was better divested
Of *all* her superfluous hair.
K.M.

To the impotent fellow from Letcher,
The lady remarked, "Glad I've metcher.
    I have long had this yen
    To erect you again—
If you find you can't come, then I'll fetcher."

H.O.

TENNESSEE

There was a young braggart from Dyer
Whose ego outstripped his desire.
    He claimed he could lay
    Twenty broads in a day.
It was only nineteen, the damn liar!
H.O.

Sought a youth from Oak Ridge, Tennessee,
A professional girl for a spree;
    But he hadn't a cent.
    Nothing daunted, he went
And seduced her one night she was free.
K.M.

A saucy young maiden of Jackson,
Though innocent-looking, and flaxen,
    When the milkman had failed,
    With her still unimpaled,
Then suggested, "Why not try the back, son?"

H.O.

There's a girl in Milan, Tennessee,
Who will lay any jocko for free,
    Like Trelawney, or Pete,
    Or that guy down the street,
Or with anyone (dammit!) but me.

K.M.

A superior girl of Savannah
Has affected an elegant mannah,
    But her favorite sport
    Of the fantasy sort,
Is to squish an erotic banannah!

K.M.

TEXAS

Said a dumb electrician of Texas,
"I perceive that the essence of sex is,
    Not so much to seduce
    As to turn on the juice
When I plug in the thing that connects us."

K.M.

A 'maso' of old Amarillo
For his fantasies uses a pillow,
    And will lie there and moan,
    With a shuddering groan,
"Give me willow, tit, willow, tit, willow!"

K.M.

A timid young fellow from Austin
Was frightened, but finally faustin;
    And after a day
    Of some copular play
Agreed it was nice, but exhaustin'.

H.O.

A team playing baseball in Dallas
Called the umpire a turd, out of malice.
    While that worthy had fits
    The team made eight hits
And a girl in the bleachers named Alice.

Anon.

A prospector who lives out in Dallas
Lays a claim to the world's largest phallas.
    But a guy in Fort Worth
    Has the biggest on Earth—
Twenty inches of uncontrolled mallas.

H.O.

In a Texas bordel, near where Dallas is
Where a tough women's libber named Alice is
    All the ladies regard
    It increasingly hard
To subscribe to those masculine phallacies.

K.M.

At a derelict brothel near Snyder
When a customer would not bestride her;
    She turned them arount
    And announced "I shall mount!"
Whence it follows the whorse was the rider.

H.O.

An inflated young husband from Hurst
Once erected himself, till he burst,
    And although it was plain
    That he suffered much pain,
It was reckoned his wife came off worst.

H.O.

For this tart from the streets of Laredo
All the cowpokes were eager to pedo,
    Since that time when her sly
    Pimping husband came by—
And they speedily made her a wedo.
K.M.

A rapacious old broad of Paducah
Is in love with the lustre of lucre
    Which she makes, wall-to-wall,
    'Cause she'll handle it all,
Whether midget or army bazooka.
K.M.

A reverend from Wichita Falls
Inadvertantly swallowed his balls,
    Thus attracting to prayer
    All the birds of the air
In response to his falsetto calls.
H.O.

UTAH

Brigham Young wasn't ever a neutah,
A pansy, a fairy or fruitah;
    Where ten thousand virgins
    Succumbed to his urgins,
We now have the great state of Utah.

LURE of the Limerick

A lady programmer from Utah
Fell in love with her handsome computah,
    And when hot with desire
    Encompassed its wire—
Which speedily rendered her neutah.

H.O.

A babe from American Fork
Could diddle before she could tork.
    Now she's in the U.K.
    And the Englishmen say,
"Wow! Can that American fork!"

H.O.

VERMONT

A hippie who lived in Vermont,
When arrested for filling the font,
    To the magistrate said,
     "The old values are dead!
We are free now to pee where we want."

K.M.

A frustrated young miss from Montpelier
In response to her paramour's felier,
    Shouted, "Let us change role.
    I bequeath you my hole
And you give me your thing—I'll impalier!"

H.O.

VIRGINIA

To this bashful young maid from Virginia
The machismo displayed his insignia
  And he said, "Be a sport;
  Though it's Virgin for short
Sure it won't be for long, once I'm inia!"

          H.O.

A liberal lady from Blakes
Has a passion for sinuous snakes,
  But will offer her tail
  To a worm, or a whale
Or do anything else that it takes.

          H.O.

In observing the mores of Norfolk,
From the rich, upper crust to the pore folk,
    I would say they've agreed
    On the obvious need
For continued production of more folk.
K.M.

An angry young maiden from Susan
Complained that her boyfriend was usin'
    A stinking old sock
    To muffle his cock
Which she thought neither safe nor amusin'.
H.O.

Said a sensitive youth of Virginia
To his paramour, "Once I beginia
    You will have no regret
    That I tend to forget
About everything else, once I'm inia."
K.M.

WASHINGTON

A Lolita from near Anacortes
Had a pref'rence for men in their forties;
    And measured at leisure
    The length of each pleasure
From tip to the curlies and shorties.

H.O.

A lady realtor of Kent
Was bearing a house sign, "For Rent."
    A handsome young joker
    Attempted to poke her—
Quite pleasant, but not what she meant.

H.O.

A frustrated bride of Seattle
Grew bored of his husbandly prattle
    And, baring her person,
    Was inwardly cursin',
"If this doesn't work, maybe that'll."

K.M.

An aggressive young girl of Spokane
Was determined to pee like a man,
    But when put to the test
    She responded, at best,
As a woefully poor also-ran.

K.M.

There was a young man of Seattle
Who bested a bull in a battle.
    With fire and with gumption
    He assumed the bull's function
And deflowered a whole herd of cattle.

Legman

A pubescent young man of Spokane
When nocturnal emissions began,
    Being ever so clean
    (Though he thought it obscene)
Would just swallow his pride like a man.

K.M.

An unpopular star from Tacoma,
Every time that he hammers a homer,
    Lets fly at the bleachers
    With asinine features
And highly unpleasant aroma.
H.O.

WEST VIRGINIA

There was once an old fellow of Welch
Who in serious moments would belch,
    Till his wife set him straight
    With a clout on the pate
And a "Button your upper—or elch!"
K.M.

An affectionate madam of Wheeling
Has no trouble her passion revealing,
    And can rise quite above
    The effusion of love
With, at bottom, a warm fellow feeling.
K.M.

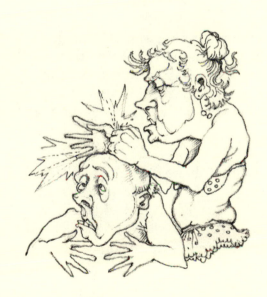

WISCONSIN

A timid young wife of Kenosha
Was frightened her husband would squash her,
　　So what did she do
　　But shorten his screw
By the use of a large metal washer.
H.O.

I remember a girl in Milwaukee,
Who would render me lustily caukee
　　As she fondled and fiddled
　　And dawdled and diddled
And other erotic malaukee.
K.M.

I would love to begin the beguine
With that ravishing girl from Racine
　　Of the smoldering eyes
　　And voluptuous thighs,
And that delicate fuzz in between.
K.M.

An exhausted young man from Sheboygan
To his girl said, "I simply can't goygan!"
　　Nothing daunted, said she,
　　"Well it's now up to me
To rekindle some life in that oygan."
K.M.

There was a young man from Racine,
Who invented a fucking machine.
     Concave or convex,
     It would suit either sex
With attachments for those in between.

Legman

That unstoppable tart of Sheboygan
Muttered, "Dammit, I'm starting to floygan
     Let me clean up the mess
     With the hem of my dress,
Then I think I'll be ready to goygan."

R.A.M.

WYOMING

An impotent monk from Cheyenne
Achieved levitation through Zen;
    And with prospects of fun
    A delighted old nun
Was encouraged to whisper, "Amen!"
H.O.

A neurotic young maid from Gillette
Thought her boyfriend a bit of a threat;
    So she stuffed her desire
    With a coil of barbed wire
And he hasn't got through to her yet.
H.O.

I recall a young lady of Laramie
Who insisted she wanted to maramie,
     But I fled in disgrace,
     For her vaginal space
Would have needed some two or three paramie.

K.M.

EDUCATIONAL INSTITUTIONS

A young polo-player of Berkeley
Made love to his sweetheart berserkeley.
    In the midst of each chukker
      He'd break off and fuck her
Horizontally, laterally and verkeley.

Legman

An unmusical person at Duke
Suffered hell to excel on the uke,
    An ambition not shared
      By a friend, who declared,
"If you don't give it up I will personally
    see to it that you are given my
      longest and strongest rebuke!"

K.M.

When a musical student of Berkeley
Made it known he'd a taste for the quirkily,
    His betrothed made it clear,
    As the moment drew near,
She preferred it legato to jerkily.
                                    K.M.

Said a scholar enrolled at Concordia
To the harlot, "I cannot affordia."
    At which she got mad
    And, with all that she had,
Started pelting his person with ordia.
                                    H.O.

A graduate at M.I.T.
Is guilty of impIET—
    Making mystical sign,
    Changing water to wine,
And saying he's God ALMIT.
                                    H.O.

A student at P.S. Tacoma
Was awarded a special diploma
    For his telling apart
    Of a masculine fart
From a similar female aroma.
                                    Legman

A sophomore student at Reed
From perversity rather than need,
    Likes to caper about
    With his wang hanging out
And in general scatter his seed.

H.O.

There isn't a choosier lay
Than Lucy at U.C.L.A.
    Just once when a horse
    Subdued her by force
Was she willing to go all the way.

H.O.

A plaintive young bugger from Yale
Was denied application for bail.
    Wrapped up in a parcel
    He posted his arcel—
It's jail to send tail by the mail.
H.O.

On the breasts of a harlot of Yale
Was emblazoned the price of her tail
    And on her behind,
    For the sake of the blind,
Was the same information in Braille.
Anon.

An erotic young doll at Penn State
Used to hand it around on a plate,
  And she muttered in haste,
  Though she liked to be chaste,
To escape was a death worse than fate.
*   H.O.*

There was once a young man from Purdue
Who was only just learning to screw;
  But he hadn't the knack
  And he got too far back—
In the right church but in the wrong pew!
*   Anon.*

An impulsive cadet from West Point
Had his nose rather put out of joint
  When its curious tip
  Was held fast in the grip
Of the thing that he hoped to annoint.
*   H.O.*

AMERICANA

Now what in the world shall we dioux
With the bloody and murderous Sioux
    Who some time ago
    Took to arrow and bow
And raised such a hullabalioux?
Eugene Field

A medicine man of the Sioux
Used to color his features bright blioux.
    When asked why he dyed,
      "Cause my squaw," he replied,
"Likes to look at the sky when we scrioux."
H.O.

Such a symbol of stud we derive
From the cult of the Colt .45,
    For its genital shape
    Sends us guys kind of ape,
With that hard, North American drive!
                   K.M.

Like that lusty young cowboy, McGraw,
Who's abnormally quick on the draw,
    And in spring, at his peak,
    Can go on for a week
At the rate of a dozen an aw.
                K.M.

Well, the bloody and murderous Sioux
As a stereotype is untrioux,
    Though they did take a stand
    In defence of their land
Making quite a tioux-dioux, wouldn't yioux?
                K.M.

Mark Twain was a mop-headed male
Whose narratives sparkled like ale;
    And the prince of the grin
    Who once fathered Huck Finn
Can still hold the world by the tale.
          Lure of the Limerick

The Mayflower's minute immigration
Appears to have peopled this nation;
    Which in turn would suggest
    That the Pilgrims at best
Were a people of fast fornication.

H.O.

To beat up the red-coated British
Was Washington's principal fitish,
    Compounding the follies
    Of Gen'ral Cornwallis
With tactics King George thought quite shitish.

H.O.

To the French our cuisine is a joke.
They dismiss us as primitive folk.
    And forget we're unique in
    (Gastronomic'lly speakin')
Kentucky Fried Chicken and Coke.

H.O.

Let us join in an anthem of gloria
In praise of the Waldorf Astoria,
    Where it's nicer to sin
    Than a Holiday Inn—
How I fervently wish they'd biltmoria!

H.O.

The longest struck ball—lie or truth—
Is of course in the records of Ruth.
        While batting in Maine
        He hit onto a train
And it traveled nonstop to Duluth.

H.O.

There was a young girl named Ann Heuser
Who swore that no man could surprise her,
        But Pabst took a chance,
        Found a Schlitz in her pants
And now she is sadder Budweiser.

Lure of the Limerick

And American music now thrives,
In our concerts of Copland and Ives—
        Such a wide social span
        From the time it began
In those sleazy bordellos and dives!

K.M.

In the conquest of space that is ours,
Observe the display of our powers—
        By dropping, like mannah,
        The star-spangled bannah
On various innocent stars.

H.O.

How cruel are the workings of fate,
As Nixon found out much too late.
    He sure didn't oughta
    Have muddied the water
Or tried to unstraiten the Gate.
H.O.

Said a drunken old man of the press,
"Our political system's a mess.
    If I wasn't so stinkin'
    I'd write to Abe Lincoln
But cannot recall his address."
H.O.

That two thousand yards of O.J.'s
Was a record that none would erase.
    But turn loose the juice—
    It may be no use
On account of the way Payton plays.
                      H.O.

There was Roosevelt's tax-saving cuts
And Kennedy's biting rebuts.
    But a Southern self-starter
    Called Carter was smarter—
He got where he is on his nuts.
                      H.O.

The West, in a tumult of chaos,
Fell in the Pacific's embraos.
    When it afterwards came
    To apportioning blame
The fault was presumed San Andreas.

H.O.

When Ehrlichman, Haldeman, Dean
And Nixon were still on the scene,
    The word of the hour
    In the corners of power
Was that men should be heard but obscene.

H.O.

Thus our praise for America northers—
Though to horrified mothers and forthers
    We are doubtless disgraced
    By insensitive taste
And such habits of limerick orthers.

Should you think we could never defend
These effusions, collected and penned
    As we bid you adieu
    We could say—shame on you
To have followed us through to

THE END !

Hugh Oliver, born in Epsom, England, came to Canada in 1966. He is editor, author, record lyric writer (the Beatles did backing music for one) and sculptor.

Keith MacMillan, born in Toronto to a family that knew 6/8 from 2/4, wrote, directed and acted in musical comedies at the University of Toronto before embarking on careers as producer of music programs for the Canadian Broadcasting Corporation, pioneer in Canadian LP and stereo recording, promoter of Canadian music (and other titillating Canadiana). Currently a solid academic.